I Wonder, Can You See Me?

Cecilia Evette

ISBN 979-8-89428-271-8 (paperback)
ISBN 979-8-89428-272-5 (digital)

Christian Faith Publishing
832 Park Avenue
Meadville, PA 16335
www.christianfaithpublishing.com

Printed in the United States of America

Contents

Section 3

First and foremost, I thank God who is my life and the very reason I have purpose and the will to pour out and be free.

To my son, Terrell Treleaven; my mother, Brenda McMichael; my brother, Ebony Gatewood; my sisters, Zanda Gatewood and Senella Baldwin; my nieces, Amina Furqan and Ayeasha Furqan-Hawkins; and nephew, Ijaz Furqan—all who motivated me to not give up and to continue to press in, I love each of you for your support.

To my circle of supportive friends—Anastasia, Daisy, Margie, Michael, and Freddie—thank you for your encouragement.

To my pastor, Alphonso Hawkins and lady Marti Hawkins, and my church family at Divine Love Christian Center COGIC, thank you for allowing my gift to flourish amongst you.

And many thanks to all of you reading my first release, *I Wonder, Can You See Me?*

As I live my day-to-day life, I sometimes wonder, Can you see me?
Can you see my hurt, can you see my wounds?
Better yet, can you see my tears?
My heart is weary and needs rest from the tearing,
the pulling, the sadness, and the fear.

I Wonder, Can You See Me?

I feel at times that I'm all alone seeking just a
release to shout, to cry, to even smile.
My surroundings make me want to hide,
run, and even disappear.
Should I feel this way, or should I stand and
just stare at it right in the face?
Should I allow the enemy to set me in chains, run my
mind, and captivate my dreams and purpose?
Will I ever get control of it all, or will I run and hide
from the bully that thinks he can run my life?

I Wonder, Can You See Me?

As I cry from deep within where it is cold, it is dark;
it is far in a dry place where no one comes.
I incline my ears just to hear a whisper. Is anyone out there?
I can't see where I am; I've lost my voice and can't even shout.

My tears are filled with all the pain and hurt
that comes from my very soul.
I search for the joy that once filled my soul.
The joy that warms me, the joy that fulfills me.

I Wonder, Can You See Me?

I wonder how and why I am here, but I know there
is a reason, and I won't be here but for a time.
I want to come out, but I feel weak and very exhausted;
my wounds have begun to heal, and the tears are
drying up, but I still can't open my eyes.
I remember what it is like to see, I remember what it is like to
walk and move around, but now I feel as though I am lame.
I keep myself in the sane place in my heart where I have hidden
my source of strength, my source of love, and my source of
life where I can begin to heal and have hope to live again.

I Wonder, Can You See Me?

I want to be better; I want to be stronger; I want to be
wiser, but more than anything, I want to love me.
I have hidden myself from me; I realize that I am in
this place because I trained myself to hide.
Now I must come out, I must stand up and dust myself
off, I need to smile at myself, and I need to love me.

I Wonder, Can You See Me?

As I am in this place, I wonder, Can I see me as a virtuous
woman worth more than rubies, silver, or gold?
I wonder, Can I see me as more than a conqueror
standing strong and wise in the Lord able to stand
even when the ground shakes beneath me?
I wonder, Can I see me as the prize a man finds in a wife to care
for myself enough to be the strength for my family again?

I wonder, Can I see me with dove eyes like the Lord does,
forgiving myself for staying in this place so long?
I wonder, Can I see me past all this rubble and destruction
and just pick up the pieces that the Lord guides me to—
pieces of love, joy, peace, longsuffering, kindness, faithfulness,
gentleness, and self-control—so I can grow in great healing?

I Wonder, Can I See Me?

Standing upright, smiling, confident and loving me again.
I wonder, Can I see beyond what is seen and focus on what is
unseen and strive for the purpose that is set before me once again?

I See Me…

Living through this, living past this, living well
beyond this part in my journey, I see me living to
witness that you can live through this too.
The wonderful thing through this is that I know I will
live again; I can spread my wings and glide through
the sky with a peace that I've never had before.
As I continue my journey, Lord, my God, bless
those who cross my path with strength to survive
whatever storm they are going through.

I Can See Me, Can You?

Leave It!

A cleansing of the land will take place.

Things that have hindered and held me captive I must leave…

As we walk into the promises of God, we are commanded
to leave those things that have hindered us, those
things that have captivated our time, our peace, our
joy, our compassion for others, and our faith.
We have been promised the best that God can give us if
we are willing to give up those things that have been part
of us for so long, things that have hurt us and have torn us
down but because they are familiar, we were captivated and
drawn to continue to give in, but now it is time to…

Leave it!

I will inherit peace that surpasses all understanding
when I admit that I can't lean on my own wisdom.
When I pray expectantly that when God's spirit
abides, I can worship in total freedom.
When I choose not to let my situations overshadow
the blessings the Lord has in store for me.
When I see past brokenness and the things that
have captivated my peace, I see my worth as I am
free I will inherit peace when I choose to…

Leave it!

I will inherit joy this world can't take away when I see beyond
the natural and gain spiritual sight. When I pray to be more and
more like God shining through darkness like a bright light.
When I understand my desires have changed for carnal
to eternal, which will last far beyond this life.
When I can share the overflow in my praise, my
worship, my humility, and even in my sacrifice,
I will inherit joy when I choose to…

Leave it!

I will inherit the greatest relationship one can
imagine when I submit myself to God's will.
When I pray for a newness each day, one that will
continue to mold me to receive God's fill.
When I understand that God's kingdom is far more important
than any kingdom built by man. When I recognize that nothing
can come to pass except when it is released from God's hand.
I will inherit the greatest relationship when I make
up in my mind to leave all my troubles behind.
And allow the cleansing to take place because I choose to leave it!

He asked me, "Son of man, can these bones live?"
I said, "Sovereign Lord, you alone know."
Then he said to me, "Prophesy to these bones and say
to them, 'Dry bones, hear the word of the Lord!
This is what the Sovereign Lord says to these bones: I will
make breath enter you, and you will come to life.

—Ezekiel 37:3–5 (NIV)

Speak Life

Can these dry bones live through trials and
tribulations that last for years and years?
Can these dry bones live through destruction
that has left us powerless and hopeless?
Can these dry bones live through heartache,
pain, and disappointments?
Can these dry bones live through dark
places that seem to have no life?

Speak life.

These dry bones can live because of the
instruction from the Lord to speak life.
These dry bones can live because of the faith
kept that is strengthened by the Lord.
These dry bones can live because of the obedience from
God's chosen people who will submit to his will.
These dry bones can live because of the latter
generations that will need guidance and teaching.

Speak life.

These dry bones will live because the Lord has instructed
for his purpose to be fulfilled in this earth.
These dry bones will live as God's chosen people
rise and repent and turn from wickedness.

These dry bones will live to give testament that God's
word is true and his grace is everlasting that many
will be freed, delivered, and made whole.
These dry bones will live because of the spoken truth given by
the Lord to the chosen who will speak life, remain humble,
have compassion, seek his face and his will for the people,
stand and believe that life can and will be restored to those who
stand in faith and expect change to overcome those dead places
and dead situations—so live because God commands us to

Speak life.

That we will live powerful and faithful through
the breath of life given by our God.

I Am a Living Testimony

You are my Savior the Prince of peace,
Lord of lords, and King of kings.
You are my Safety, my Hope, my Strength,
my Joy, you are my Everything.
I cried tears of sorrow, from heartache and pain.
But through you, the greatest love, joy, and peace I have gained.
You gave me peace and understanding to see my worth.
With the purpose you have given me that I will birth.
You are my Lord, my King, and my Source.
I will declare it with a loud voice.
I am a living testimony.
When storms are raging with no clear sight.
And mourning and sorrow throughout the night.
I will praise you, O Lord, for your mercy and grace.
As through it all, I have gained courage through my faith.
You are my present help each and every day.
I will humble myself to you and pray.
You are Victory over my challenges, Strength in my weakness.
Power in your spirit, Healing in my pain,
and Wholeness in my brokenness.
I am a living testimony.
You've placed my enemies under my feet,
given life in my dead places.
Opened my eyes that I can see, given me hearing with
understanding, a heart that forgives, compassion for others strength
to press through, praise from my very soul, and the spirit to live.

You've made me a living testimony.

I release my fear of moving into a greater level in both the physical and spiritual aspects of my life. I release the hurt and disappointment I have and ask for forgiveness for carrying it for so long. I release a deliverance for me to be a dreamer and a receiver. I release growth and strength for not only me but those on my path. I release power for our children and healing for my family. A seeker, I am. An encourager, I am. A corrector, I am. A rock, I am. I am a dreamer.

For God's word states whatever you release (loose) on earth shall be released (loosed) in heaven (Matthew 18:18) so I release (loose) these things and leave them in the loving hands of our Lord and believe the best for the future to come that I will allow myself to be a dreamer.

I Am a Dreamer

I dream that I see past the pain, I see past the
darkness, I see past the impossible.
I see into healing, I see into strength, I see
into success, I see the possible.
I see my worth when others try to destroy me.
I see because I am a dreamer.
I dream that I hear into the distance, I hear into
hearts, I hear into fear, I hear into change.
I hear past distractions, I hear past
disappointment, I hear past failing.
I hear my beat even in the middle of a storm.
I hear because I am a dreamer.
I dream that I feel healed, I feel accomplished, I feel rebuilt.
I feel my protection, I feel my comfort, I feel my peace.
I feel my strength when many think I was weak.
I feel because I am a dreamer.

I am a dreamer because I allow the Lord to guide me through darkness, comfort me in my pain, protect me from my adversaries, pour into me a promise, show me my purpose, lift me when I fall, and call me his child.

He does this because I am a dreamer.

Settle Here and Take Cover

Seek to find me, hear me, and to see my face, as I will
cover you with my glorious mercy and grace.
Seek for the rest I have provided for you, as I will
pour out a refreshing and anoint you anew.
Seek for my compassion to overtake the land, and for
my peace and my love to rest on every man.
Seek that my spirit will rest on man to guide,
into my joy and strength you shall abide.

Abide in my will and know I will guide and protect
those who belong to me and even those who reject.
Abide in the purpose I have set over your life, and
know on your behalf I send my angels to fight.
Abide in the promises I have yet to release, and know
that your enemies can't win but leave in defeat.
Abide in your faith in me for things that are unseen,
remember in all things from me you shall glean.

Glean from the riches I have stored for those I love, all
who have acknowledged me and my father above.
Glean from the wisdom I pour out to you that seek,
because of your humility and willingness to be meek.
Glean from the harvest that has been prepared in your
favor; given because of your unwavering labor.
Glean from the pasture that is prepared for you,
to rest in my glory and to be renewed.

Renewed for my purpose and will in this land, that
I get the glory and praise from all man.
Renewed in your weakness with my strength and
power, able to withstand in the final hour.
Renewed through your trials, tribulations, and pain,
pressing through and knowing it was not in vain.
Renewed in my blood that was shed to give life to all,
greater a reward for those that answered my call.

The call to settle here and take cover in this place,
now you that seek me shall see my face.

A Peace Through the Storm

On the way through the storm as the clouds darkened and I couldn't see beyond my very self, I whispered from my secret place "Jesus, Jesus, Jesus," and I soon recognized a peace and a comfort that I didn't even have before the storm hit.

This peace was so wonderful as it reminded me that I had been **chosen** for such a time as this. It reminded me how **powerful** his will and purpose are in my life, which he and only he can preserve and protect. It reminded me of how **awesome** the outcome will be as I am strengthened to stand and not be shaken. It reminded me that my father allows me to pour out the **passion** that fills my very soul right at his feet.

It reminded me of how **extraordinary** his grace and mercy are designed just for my storm as I continue to journey through. It reminded me that his **joy** is present through and after the storm if I just keep still. It reminded me that there is a constant **uplifting** of my spirit that arises in the mist. It reminded me of how **magnificent** his touch is as it touches every situation that matters in my heart and soul.

A Peace Through the Storm

It reminded me that just a piece of his **greatness** will overcome a multitude of my pain. It reminded me of the **blessing** my coming through would be to others on my path as I journey through. It reminded me that the **closer** I get to the other side of the storm, the more I will see the beauty of his mercy and his grace. It reminded me that this could be a **peaceful** place designed just for me that I may gain rest.

It reminded me of his **awesome** purpose he is protecting in me that he won't let die. It reminded me that his **deliverance** through storms such as this is not about me but for the glory of his kingdom. It reminded me that a **life**-changing storm like this will not only make me stronger or wiser but more faithful to his will. It reminded me that I was not **poured** out and emptied for me to suffer but because I am set up by him to now receive.

It reminded me that God has an **anointed** assignment for me to fulfill, and giving up is not an option. It reminded me of how **phenomenal** his plan and purpose are for his glory and that he honors me with a part. It reminded me that yes, he is not only **great** but the perfect peace I need for such a storm like this. It reminded me that he has full **control** and that I should leave all my burdens in the storm where he will bless.

A Peace Through the Storm

It reminded me that through his **supernatural** power, nothing can harm me if I am grounded in his will. It reminded me that I am **empowered** by his Holy Spirit and driven by his purpose and will for my life. It reminded me to be **expectant** that many more storms as well as blessings are coming my way. It reminded me how **peaceful** the storm really is if, like everything commanded around me, I also keep still.

The peace through the storm is none other but Jesus, Jesus, Jesus as he continues to remind me that because of my faith through this storm, this day I am being restored from pain, I am being rebuilt from brokenness, I am refreshed because **Jesus is the Peace through the storm. God bless!**

I can't look back and keep captivating myself with those things
that placed me in a spiritual prison but challenge myself to
embrace the change within and the unknown as I move forward.

I have a promise to go and get and the only option for me
is to move forward by shedding all the old things, pushing
through the obstacles and like the Israelites shout as victory
has overcome my past so I can dwell in the promise for my
present and the future to come. I will no longer die in my past
but live today and forever as I shout. I will live and not die,
for I am no longer mute, blind, deaf, or lame. I have
liberty in the promise set up before me by my father.

I will rise when I fall, dust myself off, and fight if I
have to because today I see that I have gained strength,
I have gained peace, I have gained joy and love within myself.
So no way am I going to lay that down again and allow
myself to be bullied, misled, torn, or imprisoned as I move
forward on my journey. I choose to use these very things
(strength, peace, joy, and love) as my armor and my refuge.

I choose to leave behind sickness that tried to take
over my body, being forsaken, being saddened by
things I had no control over. I also choose to move
FORWARD into the promise set before me.

I WILL MOVE FORWARD!

Move Forward

Standing still and waiting is no longer an
option, for it is time to arise and see
That the blessings and promises are far much
greater in store and waiting for me
I only must agree to not look back or worry
about those things left behind
For they are the very things that held me
captive, wounded, mute, and blind
For I am commanded to

Move forward

Through forgiveness that heals from the
root within that is buried deep
With the willingness to let go of failure
and pain I don't want to keep
The forgiveness that starts the healing and deliverance of oneself
No longer bound up with pain from others
that choose not to examine themselves
For I am commanded to

Move forward

Through weakness built strong by accepting
that I can't do it on my own
For through my brokenness and willingness,
I am delivered of all strongholds

I am rebuilt and repurposed by God's
perfection and molded in his grace
I know this day as I arise, I will live more
differently and move at a greater pace
For I am commanded to

Move forward

Through loving-kindness showered
unconditionally from our father above
With assurance, with belief, with power, and
with never-ending and agape love
For as he commands me to move forward into
the will and destiny he has just for me
Never looking back because I have a life to live
as the woman God created me to be
So as commanded, I choose to move forward so
I can see how purposed God sees me

Change in Me

Create in me a clean heart, O God; and
renew a right spirit within me.

—Psalm 51:10 (KJV)

A Change in Me
I embrace this time of change for the building
of God's kingdom and his perfect will
He will use me, he will trust me, so I will trust in him and stand still
Still enough to allow his complete work to manifest in me
No matter how hard it will be, I continue to believe God to be
My Strength while I am broken, my Comfort while I am alone,
my Joy in the midst of pain, my Shield against my enemies, my
Hope in the midst of darkness, and the Victory that I will gain

A Change in Me
My flaws and brokenness have made me who I am,
being molded into God's promise of who I will be
I will change my desires to line up with God's will and
will look at myself and be honest about what I see
I see me wanting a change and wanting to
move forward without me pulling back
I hand over to God my gifts and talents
and even what I believe I lack
Because my thoughts were clouded with my
failures, causing me to stand in a dark place

But my journey will be brighter today as I embrace
my change and everything I will have to face
As victory will come because I am willing to change, not
in my will, but for the kingdom of God to gain
I am willing to be changed!

Beautiful Butterfly

Butterfly flying high, cascading your beauty in the sky
Out of your cocoon, with liberty to soar,
with endless treasures to explore
Yellow, pink, blue, purple, shades of brown,
there is no other like you around
You display a beauty more precious than diamonds and
rings for you're a daughter of the highest king
Confident, strong, and proud, even your silence shouts out loud
Timeless, unique, and bold, a mystery you are as you unfold
You're fearfully and wonderfully designed
with a special purpose in mind
With a destiny full of joy and love because
you are one of God's beloved

You're a beautiful butterfly

I Am the Essence

Of truth that is one you can lean on and depend
You can count on me to be your closest and dearest friend
I never take it lightly the time and tears we share
For when you are going through, I will hold
up your hands so you can bear
I carry this treasure important and dear in my soul
I am the essence of truth one you can behold

I am the Essence
Of faith as I rise above all adversity and pain
For I know I must press through the valley
because I have so much to gain
My faith can move mountains and even
pull me up when I am down
I started with just a small mustard seed,
but I planted it in the ground
My faith is rooted deep in my belief in God, it
is covered by his mercy and by his grace
I am the essence of faith and will not be shaken from this place

I am the Essence
I search my inner being to the very core
Finding all the beautiful treasures that God so gracefully pours
I found one called virtue for I must protect this one with grace
For this one shows my worth and purity much
greater than the beauty of my face
It will be the last part of me that I will unfold
I am the essence of virtue more precious than rubies, silver, and gold

Proverbs 31—this is my virtue as I am created to be.

*****

Whoso findeth a wife findeth a good thing,
and obtaineth favour of the Lord.

—Proverbs 18:22 (KJV)

Her Virtue

He finds in her peace, respect, understanding,
trust, and undeniable love
Treasures she gained through the molding
and perfecting from her father above
Her posture is of humility, fear, reverence,
and praise through a servant's heart
Her desire is to rest at the feet of the living
God and never be far apart

She realizes that her place of worship is a sacred place
where with the Living God she will commune
A place where she is refreshed, strengthened,
built, positioned, purposed, and renewed
Able to get God's attention on matters and
concerns from her very heart
She seeks after God's protection, his grace
and his mercy that will never depart

He will find her clothed in garments of praise and
grounded in faith through God's wisdom
Which allows her shout, praise, and prayers to tear down
walls hindering the building of God's kingdom
He will find her seeking after God's own heart, powered
through his spirit, and comforted under his grace
For she is blessed above measure from the Living God
through her obedience, patience, and faith

She gains benefits through surrendering her will as
she is covered by his blood so love can unfold
He that finds this virtue will love and cherish
her more than rubies, silver, or gold
Her beauty is illuminated through her posture in
God's purpose as his spirit shines through
He that finds this virtue shall gain blessing
in his household forever true…
Because this is her virtue

May God continue to shower you with his abundant
blessings to stand strong, unmovable, and loved by all
I am blessed because in you, I see me and what I am created to be

Mother

Created from the rib of man to be the nourisher of
all generations from the beginning till the end
You were created to be the mother of the earth,
and from you all generations will be birthed
You'll birth kings and queens, husbands, and wives;
so the choices you make will affect all lives, You'll
pour out love that heals, protects, and provides as
you're equipped through the purpose inside
You'll pour out wisdom, strength, and even pain for
all generations and the kingdom of God to gain

Mother

With great responsibility and power to hold;
with no excuses, so stand up bold
Responsible for what this world will see, you're the
foundation used to build and mold to be
Emulated rather than defeated or proud, weak, or strong,
bold, or meek; guidance from you will all seek
Your essence will overflow into the hearts and minds and
will be remembered from the beginning of time
All battles you'll face, no matter how big or small, are
already won; so hold your head up and stand up tall
Remember who you are and to whom you belong; for
the purpose within will help you travel along

Mother

The journey you've taken will not be forgotten or lost; nor will the
battles that you have fought. Through darkness, evil, heartache, and
even pain; your sacrifice never wavered so now you have gained
Faith unshaken, joy through sorrow; peace through
storms, and blessings for tomorrow
You've built a legacy on faith, prayers, resilience,
strength, and love; to ensure a life spent up above
With God's abundant blessings showered from
heaven above, for you are chosen as his beloved
Now this day, your children will lift you up so you can shine
For you are mother of all time

Her children arise up, and call her blessed;
Her husband also, and he praiseth her.

—Proverbs 31:28 (KJV)

We Shall Call Her Blessed

Momma, Mom, Mommy, Mother—we shall call her blessed
Blessed to stand strong like an unmoving tower
Blessed to symbolize the pillars of strength,
wisdom, counsel, and power
Blessed to be able to care for each of her children
with poured out favor from above
Blessed to endure the pain of disappointment and continue
to carry on with strength and love. Blessed to be able to smile
at adversities and stand strong in the midst of a storm
Blessed to claim her territory to create a legacy
for her children to follow and carry on

We shall call her blessed
Blessed to have arms that spread wide enough
to comfort any hurt or pain
Blessed to stand still and root herself in
what she believes she will gain
Blessed to share wisdom to provide her
children with courage to survive
Blessed to have the strength to encourage even when sadness abides
Blessed to see past all the imperfections and
lean on God's mercy and grace
Blessed to feel compassion even when tears run down her face

We shall call her blessed
Blessed to hear her children's hearts even
when words aren't expressed
Blessed to love past failure, hurt and brokenness

Blessed to be the root that grounds her family's love
Blessed to be called one of God's beloved
Blessed to lift others even when she is down
Blessed to believe that one day she will receive a glorious crown
Momma, Mom, Mommy, Mother—as you triumph above the rest
We stand and call you blessed

*As I continue to lean on the Lord for strength, guidance,
protection, knowledge, and his everlasting love, I will hold my
head up and let him lead me in the most beautiful dance.*

I Want to Dance

I have stumbled and fell as I tried to keep
my feet planted on the ground
"Move," he says. "It will be okay. Just take one
step at a time, and don't look down
I will guide you. Hold my hand, and just follow
my lead. I won't let you stumble or fall
Keep your back straight, and your head up, and stand up tall
I will lead you into the most peaceful and beautiful
journey that you could ever imagine
But you must move your feet and trust in me
You must trust that I will provide strength to
hold you with every step and as you turn
You must trust that I will provide a path that you can follow
You must trust that I have your best interest in
my thoughts and very dear to my heart
You must trust that I want to let you display your beauty and love
You must trust that I don't want you to fail but prevail
You must trust that I will give you all that I can
You must trust that I desire for you to dance

Cecilia, can I have this dance?"

And thou shalt love the Lord thy God with all thine
heart, and with all thy soul, and with all thy might.

—Deuteronomy 6:5 (KJV)

I Love the Lord My God

Love the Lord, thy God, with all thine heart…

I love the Lord my God with all my heart; his word
I shall treasure that it shall never depart
As it is my safety and my peace; so my faith
in him continues to increase
That I shall not be moved or even shaken; for in
my heart, I know I am never forsaken
I am set free from all sickness and pain; with
eternal life through Christ, I gain

Love the Lord thy God with all thy soul…

I love the Lord my God with all my soul; a
gentle touch from him makes me whole
In my truth, where I can worship and praise, for
all his miracles that some are amazed
That even in the midst of my tribulations, my
soul declares him great for all generations
For he is the same today, tomorrow, and
forevermore, with his everlasting love in store

Love the Lord Thy God with all thy might…

I love the Lord my God with all my might;
so I walk by faith and not by sight
Into the promises he has declared for me,
that in Christ I shall live abundantly

In my coming in and my going out, "Hallelujah"
and "Glory to God" I will shout
For all the blessings and favor he has shown toward
me and how he has truly set me free

I Love the Lord my God

Pressed is defined as "to move or cause to move into a position of contact with something by exerting continuous physical force."

Position is defined as "a place where someone or something is located or has been put."

Purpose is defined as "the reason for which something is done or created or for which something exists."

Promise is defined as "a declaration or assurance that one will do a particular thing or that a particular thing will happen."

Pressed into Position for the Purpose in the Promise

I am pressed to rise and believe in the purpose that is already in me. I must open my heart and allow my mind to grasp the good thing the Lord has placed and is protecting in me. I will no longer be bound to apologize for the greatness purposed for me and through me as I allow the Lord to shine his light and expose his promise for all to see. The pressing has placed in me a hunger and thirst after righteousness, where I must die to my will and, in obedience, follow God's instructions as I am pressed into position.

Positioned for a great work to take place, for by no means will I move into the promise without preparation. I am commanded, while in position, to be honest about those things that concern me. Like the Israelites, I must meditate on the matters of my heart, for when the alarm is sounded, my shout is exalted to the heavens from the depths of my very being so that every wall that has stood about has fallen down, doors are now opened, and by the instructions from the Lord, I shall walk right into the promise where there is an overflow, an increase, and a purpose destined just for me.

The purpose God created for me before the foundation of this world—one molded on this earth for the perfection in heaven. A purpose that causes a purification, which promotes the filling of the anointing, which enables me to journey through with the greatest treasures. Treasures that only God can pour in, those of love, joy, peace, longsuffering, gentleness, goodness, faith, meekness, and temperance. These things shall endure the fire, weather any storm, and promote the overflow in the promise.

God gave the Israelites led by Moses and Joshua the Promised Land where flowing milk and honey awaited, so what more is waiting for me through the blood of Jesus? I am made a new vessel, stretched and molded by the hand of God, filled with his anointing, restored with his power because of my obedience to his will.

I am pressed into position for the purpose in the promise through Jesus's blood to have everlasting life.

Shout

This decree is not just any decree but one
that will surely set you free
It dwells in the core of your very soul, from the
tears and pain that have taken their toll
Its roots are buried deep and bring much sorrow,
but rest in the promises for tomorrow
The promise of **joy** this world can't take away
and new **mercy** given to you every day
The promise of **love** that covers a multitude of
sin, a new **life** given for you to begin
In the midst of depression, do not fear, but
be still enough for you to hear
The angels' wings and the trumpets blast, THEN
Shout down depression and be free at last
Remembering the promise that God will set the captives
free, so you, through Christ, are free indeed
If loneliness has overtaken you, know the
friend you have in Jesus is forever true
Hear in your heart that you are not alone, THEN
Shout down loneliness and stand up bold
On the promise that he hath said, "I will never
leave thee, nor shall I forsake thee"
If a stronghold has you bound, fast and pray
for your release and stand your ground
Believing that, on your behalf, God will fight, THEN
Shout down strongholds with all your might
Declaring no weapon formed against you shall prosper or stand,
for the enemy and his tactics will be given into your hands

Shout, for you are the **head** and not the tail,
and through Christ, you shall prevail
Shout, for you are **first** and not last; move
into your future and leave the past
Shout, for you are **fearfully** and **wonderfully**
made; with a purpose from God
that won't fade
Shout, for you are more than a **conqueror,** and there is no **defeat**;
Shout straight into your victory!

And it shall come to pass afterward, that I will pour out my spirit upon all flesh; and your sons and your daughters shall prophesy, your old men shall dream dreams, your young men shall see visions.

—Joel 2:28 (KJV)

Receive the Pouring

Set forth to tear down, to restore, to make whole, to fulfill,
to strengthen, and to edify the kingdom of God
The pouring that promised a healing that expands from generation
to generation when repentance is in the hearts of the people
The pouring that will give our sons and daughters
prophecy from their lips and our young men
visions no man has ever seen or spoken
The pouring established way back on Calvary
through the blood of the Lamb that by our faith,
we are free and not bound to a desolate land

Receive the pouring

That allows us to live a full and everlasting life through
his grace and glide freely on the wings of his mercy
The pouring that fallows the land to be prosperous in and out
of harvest for the gain of those of rich and those of poor
The pouring that opens eyes that they will see, ears that they will
hear, strengthens the lame to walk, and softens hearts to receive
The pouring that can only be accomplished by the spoken
word and the spirit of the Lord of lords and King of kings

Receive the pouring

As it flows on us when we believe in his living, share of his return,
die to our flesh, seek his face, acknowledge his will, be obedient
in his instruction, stand in faith, receive of his power, trust in
his glory, follow his path, and have compassion for all people.

Receive the pouring of God's Spirit and echo it through the
valleys and from the mountaintops as it declares we are free

Lord, pour out your spirit that we will see your
word fulfilled in this land and walk in liberty

Receive the pouring

Not just a child, but one with a purpose
Be bold like David, faithful like the three Hebrew boys,
willing like Samuel, and one after God's heart
Do this because you're not just a child!

Not Just a Child

But chosen and set apart by the one and only living God
Purposed for a will established before the foundation of this world
Purified by his grace and washed in his love
One chosen to stand on the word and receive
understanding above and beyond your years
One who will allow the Holy Spirit to guide
from within to shake off all fears

Not just a child

But one who will seek for God's will and purpose for your life
One who will place all concerns in the hands of the Lord with
an expectation that he receives what is in your very heart
One who will seek not your own heart's
desire but one sent from above
One chosen to be a strong vessel—not broken, but whole—to pour
out to fulfill a mission greater than you can see or understand
One who presses past the courts and gets to the throne to lie down
before the Lord, knowing that all things gained come from his hand

Not just a child

But one who will stand like David and face all Goliaths
in faith that the love of God will overcome
One who knows the power of God and is willing to go in the
fire like the three Hebrew boys and come out unharmed
One like Samuel who will hear God's voice,
answer his call, and remember his strength

One who will go bold like a lion but can still be gentle as a dove
One chosen to shine bright in conduct, in
love, in faith, in purity, and in speech
One who will be part of the rising generation who will follow God's
instructions, have a heart for God's people, and seek for God's peace

Not just a child

Terrell, you are so treasured and loved in my heart
that the safest place I can provide for you is in
the comforting arms of our Living God
Rest in him, find your help and strength in him, my son
Love you forever and to the end of time

Mom

Son of the Living God

Rise from the dust, young man, and stand strong
Believe that the living God is watching and
directing, because to him you belong
He created you to be powerful, courageous, and bold
You are to build a great legacy for generations to behold
You are to see past the trouble that seems to be all around
You will stand and not be shaken because
of the faith you have found
Faith in the Living God that will never leave nor forsake
He will guide you and protect his purpose for his name's sake
He declares in his word that he shall comfort thee
So find your place in him and truly submit all that you will be
Submit all the burdens, all the hurt, all
the pain, and all the rejection
So you can find your rest surrounded by his protection
He is the Lamp at your feet that will guide you
through even the darkest of hours
So place your trust in him and gain his power
For his power defeats all enemies that rise against thee
For at his name, they all must submit, bow, and flee
He called you to rise for this generation's sake
So you must trust in what is in you and lean on all your faith
All the days won't be perfect, and troubles are
not shielded from coming your way
But stand and be of great courage on this day
Make pathways so those behind you can follow as you lead
Ask for God's wisdom, understanding and
knowledge to build you to be

It's in your asking for it comes from your very soul
The Lord our God will reveal himself in all his
might and his glory for you to grab hold
If you should feel like you can go no more
Mount up with wings of eagles so you will find
your rest, regain your strength, and soar
Soar till you renew your sight and gain God's vision
For all he has purposed in you and through
you shall prevail with his provision
He will mold you to be a man of valor who
will be unwavering and be of no fear
When you receive of his spirit that is drawing you so near
Son, on this day, reach out and grab tight; do not
let go, and hold on with all your might
Hold on till you receive all that you will need
As today I release you to be
The son of the Living God and the man
you are created and called to be

Man of God

A man with much confidence stands firm and
unmovable in what he believes and loves
He is like a roaring lion in times for protection but
can be as understanding and as gentle as a dove
His journey may seem rough and ragged, but he
overcomes it with courage and mighty strength
He rises above like an eagle and places his sight on
those things purposed and are heaven-sent
He is a man with a heart after God that
is filled with never-ending love
Able to shake off the dust from pain and hurtful
situations and still show agape love
Not moved or distracted from the corruption that tries to pull
him down or cloud his thoughts, because he has faith that
carries him through valleys and sits him on the mountaintops
He has traveled through stormy nights, some
dark days, and some troubled times
But as he stands this day with thanks in
his heart and peace in his mind
He knows where his strength came from and
leans on the wisdom he has gained
He counts it all joy and says he cannot complain
This man of God cannot be shaken or even moved
from the path set before him this day
As the path he is following will attract the lost, the
hurt, the broken, and many more on his way

A purpose far much greater than he could even see or understand
So this man of God will place his trust in God to
build him, to mold him that he will withstand

He is a true man of God…

The Courage of a Father

A father is he of great courage as he sets his
example before his household
He demonstrates humility and fear toward the Lord
our God, who helps him to stand strong and bold
His very image is emulated by his children, which places
him in a position to lean not on his own will
But to search out the understanding and perfect
will of God that his children shall fulfill

He sacrifices his desires to be shifted into a place, to
receive a desire to reap blessings for generations
Blessing that his children's children shall inherit as
they position themselves on the true foundation
The foundation that God instructed men to build on,
which weathers any storm and all tribulations
Through his tribulations, he is refined and proven to be
resilient as he stands and makes his declarations

Declarations from his mouth set him free from
captivity, pain, rejection, and even defeat
A defeat that is crafted by the enemy to not only take
him down but cause generations to retreat
His declarations show his courage, his power,
and his compassion for his legacy
A legacy that is anchored with his hope and his faith
that he places in God for a lifetime prosperity

A prosperity that will not fade, but gains in its worth
through the promises in God's word toward them
The word that says the righteous who walk in his
integrity—blessed are his children after him
Blessed because of the courage to release his heart, to
be molded into a heart for God's purpose and will
A will that grants prosperity, hope, strength, courage,
and love, that God has entrusted in him to instill
This is
The courage of a father

Surrender

"An agreement to stop fighting, hiding, resisting, etc., because you know that you will not win or succeed: an act of surrendering: the act of giving the control or use of something to someone else."

Pursue truth and righteousness above all else.
A feeling that if one more thing comes my way,
I am just going to break or collapse.
I feel like I am not myself and in an unfamiliar
space or time, and I can't shake it.

Surrender

Will you allow me to pour out my love into your heart
to mold you to the woman I created you to be?
Will you allow me to show you the wonders
of my heart and visions of my pain?
Will you allow me to comfort you in your time of pain?
Will you allow me to lift you higher than you ever been lifted before?
Will you allow me to guide you through the valleys and the plains?
Will you allow me to be the light in the depth of darkness?
Will you allow me to wipe the tears from your eyes?
Will you allow me to set the promise of peace in the skies?
Will you allow me to move mountains into
to sea and cause waters to roll back?
Will you allow me to cause the enemy to be your
footstool and cause his hand to release?
Will you allow me to be everything you have
need of and the source of your life?
Will you allow me to show you unspeakable
and undeniable miracles?
Will you allow me to be he who was sent from
heaven to take on all the world's sin?
Will you allow me to be he who sits high and looks
low, all-knowing of yesterday, today, and forever?
Will you allow me to be he who controls the sea and
the storms; and at my command, they will cease?
If you allow these things and totally surrender,
you shall have rest on every side
Because I am He who will provide
All you must do is ***surrender*** and believe me to be

A declaration in the atmosphere that can be heard
in the heavens that sends the enemy in flight,
as they cannot stand against the power flowing
from the very vessel, they were sent to fight.

*****

No weapon that is formed against thee shall prosper;
and every tongue that shall rise against thee in judgment thou
shalt condemn. This is the heritage of the servants of the
LORD, and their righteousness is of me, saith the LORD.

—Isaiah 54:17 (KJV)

SOUND OF VICTORY

The sound will move mountains into the
sea and cause all demons to flee
It will cause sickness to submit and cause
a pressing that will not quit
It is anchored with faith and has no fear as it
presses through dimensions into God's ear
It's the intercession of the Holy Spirit when the flesh
agrees that no weapon can be formed against thee
It's the sound that is created from the depth of the
soul, formed together from the moans and groans
It's the explosion that takes down stone walls, which
were created to force retreat and warriors to fall
It's the sound of the angels' wings, sent from heaven to fight for me
It's the sound that shook the whole earth when the veil
was torn, ordained before this earth was formed
The sound that filled the very space as Christ bled
and died for believers to see him face to face
It's the sound of the Lord rising from his throne to
assure me that I am not in the fight alone
It's the sound that strengthens me to fight with
praise, worship, prayers, and total sacrifice
It's the sound when the wounds have healed and
hands are set free, so in the heart is victory
The sound that declares "I am here to reclaim everything
stolen as the Lord my God has proclaimed"
The sound is risen through God's strength and power
to continue to fight through the final hour

The sound formed as the vessel is free to shout the declaration
and decree whom the Son sets free is free indeed
So today I will stand and lift my head as I am
free for all to hear my *SOUND OF VICTORY*

About the Author

Cecilia Evette was born and raised in Denver, Colorado. She is a mother of one son, Terrell Treleaven. She served in the US Army for ten years, which included a deployment to Iraq during Operation Iraqi Freedom. On her return from the thirteen-month deployment in Iraq, her life changed; the battlefield she was now on was detrimental to her survival—not her physical survival, but her spiritual survival, where just writing poetry to the physical man was no longer satisfying. Through her tribulations and brokenness, a transformation happened, causing a birthing in the spiritual realm. Here Cecilia learned to shake herself off, stand up, and live what she describes as the most rewarding life in the presence of God.

Cecilia is inspired by God when she writes. Her poetry breathes life into her, and her hope is that it will do the same for those who read it, as it is not for her personal fulfillment but for the glory of God. Cecilia will continue to allow God to speak with her and through her as she continues her journey through the releasing of *I Wonder, Can You See Me?* She is now stretching into the promises of God as her journey continues to unfold. She says she wants to be found doing what God has called and purposed her to do in this season to declare the goodness of God through the gift he has given her through writing to uplift, encourage, pull down, build up, and lead someone to God's love.

www.ingramcontent.com/pod-product-compliance
Lightning Source LLC
Chambersburg PA
CBHW021137130726
47988CB00003B/1343